THE RELUCTANT ROGUE
ROGUE
OR
MOTHER'S DAY

A PLAY
BY JOHN PATRICK

DRAMATISTS
PLAY SERVICE
INC.

SOUND EFFECTS RECORD

The following sound effects record, which may be used in
connection with production of this play, can be obtained from
Thomas J. Valentino, Inc., 151 West 46th Street, New York,
N.Y. 10036.

No. 5025 — Telephone ring

FOREWORD

This play will fail as entertainment unless the leading role is cast with an actor who is so attractive physically — who has such a devastating smile and an equally beguiling personality, that one cannot help but be captivated. And forgive him. But aware, nevertheless — that we know people like him who use their charms as lethal weapons — as frivolously as the Borgias once used their poison.

CHARACTERS

REED DOLAN
ROBERTA GUTMAN
ANGIE PEPPERDINE
INGRID NOVOTNY
HERCULES HOMER HUNTER
VANESSA JACOBS
BOY
ZENOBIA HUNTER

THE RELUCTANT ROGUE

ACT I

TIME: *The present.*
PLACE: *The bachelor apartment, just off campus, of young Professor Reed Dolan.*
AT RISE: *Reed sits at a card table, correcting a pile of term papers. He is a slim, attractive man in his early thirties with considerable animal magnetism. He is in slacks and shirt sleeves, wearing horn-rimmed eye glasses. There is a drink beside him from which he occasionally sips.*
He groans as he picks up each new bound essay.
The phone rings.

REED. Oh, shit! (*He crosses to the phone on the sofa end table.*) Hello? Oh, hello, Mother. (*He slumps down, feet up, for what he knows to be a tedious session.*) I was *just* sitting here thinking about you! How are you, sweetheart? What do you mean—*disappointed?* (*Hits his forehead.*) Oh, no! Oh, my God, don't tell me it's Mother's Day. Not *again!* Oh, darling, I'm *so* sorry I forgot. (*Sighs.*) I *know* it isn't asking too much, Mother. I *know* it only costs a postage stamp, sweetheart. I *know* you almost died when I was born, darling. I know! I know! I know! (*Straightens up.*) Wait a minute—don't hang up! Let me explain. Mother, I was in a car accident and just got out of the hospital today. I'm still on crutches. (*Crosses his legs.*) I didn't want to worry you, honey bun. Now, am I forgiven? What do you mean by—*"this time"*?

Oh, don't tell me I forgot last year, too! (*Slumps again.*) Mother, I'm a no-good bastard. I don't deserve a wonderful, understanding, uncomplaining, forgiving saint like you for a mother. You should be the mother of a President — not a half-assed teacher in a half-assed college with a half-assed memory when it comes to the most important day in his life. Darling, I promise if I forget next year, I'll kill myself. Will that make you happy? No — no! Don't hang up — I was just joking, pudding-pie. I love you. I'm looking at your picture right now. (*Looks at his drink.*) Of course I do — I keep it framed on the end table where I can always see it when I get lonely. (*Smiles with self-satisfaction.*) How's Dad? He's quit his job! *Again?* (*Sits up righteously.*) Put him on. He's what! He's gone out to a bar for a *drink!* Leaving you alone on Mother's Day? What a shit. No — I mean it. You gave up a career for that Irish slob. You could have been a famous singer. Another Barbra Streisand — God forbid. Why did he quit his job? A night watchman has a great opportunity to sleep. Yes — I'm listening. Go ahead. (*He puts the phone down and goes up to the bar to make himself another drink. He returns and picks up the phone again.*) Yes. Yes. That's terrible. I'm sure glad I take after *you,* baby — not him. Are you *sure* he's my father? No — no — don't hang up. I was just joking. Do you need any *money,* dear? Well, you can't live on Social Security and food stamps forever. Well, he's wrong. Sweetie, I'm going to send you a check anyhow. I want you to buy yourself a Mother's Day present. Something silly that you don't need. Like a stainless steel asparagus knife or a high colonic. Wait — wait! Don't hang up — I was just trying to cheer you up. I *wasn't* being sarcastic — I'm not like that. I take after *you.* Yes, Mother — I know. It's no day to be sarcastic. Anyhow, you've made *my* day by calling and I thank you from the bottom of my ungrateful heart. Well, go out and bowl or get drunk. Well, go to church then and play bingo. Thanks again for calling. Love you dearly. Kiss — kiss. Bye, bye. (*He hangs up.*) Oh, shit. (*Clasps his hands together in prayer.*) Oh, Lord — be a good sport and *at least* let me remember her *birth*day. (*Adds.*) Whenever *that* is. (*Looks around.*) Where the hell's my date book? (*Finds it.*) Mary McGuiness Doland — Mary McGuiness Dolan — here we are. Birthday — April 7th. That's about Easter. (*Throws date book aside and starts back to table.*) I'll send her a bunny rabbit. (*Sits at card table to resume work. The phone rings.*) Oh, shit! (*Crosses to answer.*) Hello. And a big wet kiss to you, too. Who is this? Oh, Annabelle! Of course I knew—I was just teasing you. Did I? Well, I *was* going to call you but my phone's been out of order. The repairman *just* left, dear. No, Duckie, I *can't* leave my *apartment* tonight, I've got a million term papers to grade. Besides, I've got a terrible cold and I wouldn't want you to catch it. I'll call you, Angel. Be good. (*Hangs up.*) Who the hell is Annabelle? God! Will they never leave me alone? (*Sips his drink and sits at card table again. Ponders.*) Annabelle? (*Shrugs.*) Oh, well. What the hell. (*Picks up an essay. The door chimes are heard.*) Oh, shit! (*Yells.*) Come in! It's not locked. (*Roberta Gutman, a pert and nubile young student enters in tight jeans.*)

ROBERTA. Am I interrupting you, Professor Dolan?

REED. (*Takes glasses off and rises.*) Not at all—not at all. (*Responds with instant charm.*) Come in. Shut the door. You must be Vanessa.

ROBERTA. Roberta. Roberta Gutman._ It's about my term paper.

REED. Of course, Roberta. Roberta Gutman. What a lovely name—no frills. Sit down, Roberta. (*She does. He puts on his jacket.*) I called you Vanessa because someone by that name called me this morning and said she'd be in to see me today. You see, I've so many drama majors this term that I get a little mixed up. I should have known *you're* not Vanessa—whoever she is. You have a much more melodic voice. Do you sing?

ROBERTA. I can't even whistle.

REED. Well, forgive a dull, doddering old professor for thinking you were someone else.

ROBERTA. You're the youngest teacher on campus, sir.

REED. If you call me "sir," you're going to make me feel the *oldest.* (*Accelerates the charm.*)

ROBERTA. Yes, sir.

REED. (*Waves a roguish finger.*) None of that, now. Call me Reed. I didn't call you *Miss* Gutman, did I?

ROBERTA. No—you called me Vanessa.

REED. Well, from now on when we talk in private—it's "Reed" and "Roberta." Agreed? Good. (*Sits beside her.*) Now, how can I help you, Roberta?

7

ROBERTA. It's about my term paper on Molière. I wasn't able to finish it in time to submit it. (*She holds out a folder.*) Will that be held against me?

REED. I would never hold anything against you that inconsequential.

ROBERTA. Oh, that makes me feel so much better.

REED. I hoped it would. (*She rises to go.*) But as long as you're here, dear, why don't you sit down and wait while I look over — (*Glances at her young bosoms.*) — your Molière.

ROBERTA. Oh, yes. I'd love to get it done in a hurry — if you have time.

REED. I always have time *not* to hurry. Would you like something to drink?

ROBERTA. No thank you.

REED. (*Disappointed.*) Well, sit down and let's get to Molière. (*They both sit on the sofa.*) Molière. I would never have thought anyone as young as you would have chosen Molière as a subject. How old are you, dear?

ROBERTA. Ancient.

REED. Oh, I doubt that. Well — Molière.

ROBERTA. I was going to pick Mendelssohn but he made me feel so inadequate. Imagine having written a couple of operas and piano sonatas before you're even seventeen.

REED. And you weren't yet seventeen?

ROBERTA. Seventeen? That's senile nowadays. Did you know Goya started painting at fourteen?

REED. Good God — you're not fourteen, are you!

ROBERTA. Heavens, no. At fourteen I was as flat-chested as my older brother.

REED. (*Shifts his position.*) You've an older brother? Here at school?

ROBERTA. No, he graduated eight years ago. He's been a police officer for five.

REED. (*Stiffens.*) A policeman?

ROBERTA. (*Nods.*) Just like my father.

REED. Oh. (*This sobers him.*)

ROBERTA. He's a captain.

REED. Oh.

ROBERTA. You might say, I've grown up in protective custody.

REED. How interesting.

ROBERTA. That's why it was such a relief to get away from their over-protective vigilance.

REED. (*Pats her hand.*) And you're quite right. When you're old enough to vote—you're old enough to make your own moral judgments. Who'd you vote for this year, dear?

ROBERTA. Bernadine Durdle.

REED. Who!

ROBERTA. Bernadine Durdle. She ran for Class President.

REED. I meant on a more *mature* level.

ROBERTA. Well, I've never thought maturity should be equated chronologically.

REED. (*Nods.*) I see you have a mind of your own.

ROBERTA. Couldn't you judge that better by reading my Molière, sir?

REED. Of course—of course. (*Picks up folder.*) Molière. (*Reads.*) "Jean Baptiste Molière was born in the year of our Lord sixteen twenty-two." (*Stops to pat her hand again.*) I like that—"in the year of our Lord." It shows a nice romantic flair.

ROBERTA. *I* thought it kind of weak and prosaic.

REED. No—no—no. You must never demean a romantic weakness. One must be strong about weakness.

ROBERTA. Isn't that a contradiction in terms?

REED. (*Rather loftily.*) *Life* is a contradiction. However, we're not making progress—with Molière. (*Rests his arm on the back of the sofa around her shoulder and reads.*) "Molière's father was the Royal upholsterer to Louis the Thirteenth, King of France." (*Lets his hand fall on her shoulder.*) Now, I didn't know that myself.

ROBERTA. It's in any Dictionary. Paperback. (*Points.*) That's the appointment in Latin. (*Reads.*) "Deo teste meo, ut Johannus Baptistus Poquelinis hinc ad munus suppelectilis regalis instruendae designaretur de manu ipsa ego Ludivicus tredecimus, rex Galliae decrevi."

REED. So I see—so I see. (*Reads the Latin aloud. Then repeats in English.*) You know what this shows, Roberta? It shows you've done your research and research shows scholarship and scholarship shows a sagacious mind. I can't believe you're only sixteen.

ROBERTA. Eighteen.

REED. (*Heartened.*) Well, now. Eighteen? Shall we get on with it?

9

ROBERTA. If you don't mind.

REED. (*Gives her shoulder a little reassuring hug.*) I don't mind at all. So many of these assignments are incredibly dull. *You've* managed to capture my interest in your very first paragraph. That shows intuitive skill.

ROBERTA. *Thank* you, Professor!

REED. (*Corrects her.*) Reed.

ROBERTA. Reed.

REED. Now. Where were we? (*Reads.*) "Molière was not the real family name. It was —" (*Turns to Roberta.*) How do you pronounce that?

ROBERTA. (*With the French accent.*) Poquelin.

REED. (*Takes her chin in his hands.*) Roberta — you astound me. You put your finger on what's basic and relevant with unerring insight.

ROBERTA. Do I? Really?

REED. (*Takes her hands.*) Don't you trust my judgment? What earthly reason would I have for subterfuge? (*Takes his hands away.*)

ROBERTA. (*Grabs his hands back.*) Oh, I didn't mean you were just being indulgent. Oh, please don't think that, Professor.

REED. (*Corrects her again.*) *Reed.*

ROBERTA. Reed.

REED. That's better. Because you're an exceptional student — the kind I'd like to take under my wing.

ROBERTA. And I'm *very* grateful. You don't know how I appreciate your interest.

REED. Good. We're going to get along just fine, Vanessa.

ROBERTA. *Roberta.*

REED. Roberta. (*Puts folder down.*) Would you like to know something?

ROBERTA. That's why I'm a student.

REED. *You* confuse me. It's your own fault that I get so distracted.

ROBERTA. What have I done?

REED. It's not what you've *done.* Heavens no. It's what you are.

ROBERTA. What are I — I mean — am I?

REED. You have the most compelling personality of all the students here this year. You walk into class and there's something about you that immediately arrests attention. Oh, don't think I haven't watched you. I'm not immune yet.

ROBERTA. Oh, Professor! I mean — Reed.

REED. And you don't help us poor mortals by wearing that intoxicating perfume. What is it?

ROBERTA. You won't like the name. I don't. But it was a Christmas present.

REED. What's it called?

ROBERTA. "Lust."

REED. Don't wear it any more, dear.

ROBERTA. I *thought* it might offend you.

REED. It's not that. You know what it should be called? "Assault With a Deadly Weapon."

ROBERTA. (*Laughs.*) I'll take a shower.

REED. No — no — no. We mustn't go to extremes. But it *is* devastating. (*He leans forward.*) It incites me into paying due homage. (*Kisses her on the forehead.*)

ROBERTA. Thank you. (*He kisses her on the lips — then pulls her to him. A struggle ensues in which he finds himself on the floor on his back.*)

REED. My God — you're strong.

ROBERTA. Dad taught me judo. (*Picks up phone.*)

REED. (*From the floor.*) What are you doing?

ROBERTA. Calling Dr. Bonds. I think our college president should know we have a sex maniac in Contemporary Drama Two.

REED. Wait! Wait! (*Scrambles up.*) Let me explain.

ROBERTA. You don't have to explain this to *me*. I took Sex Orientation as a freshman.

REED. Listen, dear — if you report me, I'll lose tenure.

ROBERTA. (*Holds phone.*) Ten years of what?

REED. No — *tenure* of office. When I've put in six more months, I can't be discharged.

ROBERTA. It's too long to wait. (*Dials.*)

REED. Please — Vanessa — *Roberta*. Do you want to kill my mother?

ROBERTA. What's your mother got to do with your libido? You should be ashamed of yourself.

REED. Please listen. Just before you came in, I got a telephone call. They were taking my mother to the hospital.

11

ROBERTA. (*Considers this.*) On Mother's Day?

REED. That's the only reason I turned to you—for a little human warmth. I just had to feel I wasn't alone.

ROBERTA. What's wrong with your mother—outside of having whelped you.

REED. Don't be unkind, Roberta. I'm going thru hell at the moment. (*He sits on the sofa and buries his head in his hands.*) Don't you understand? I *needed* you.

ROBERTA. I'm not your mother.

REED. And *I'm* not important myself. But to add to *her* pain at a time like this—is something I can't bear. Don't hurt her more. She struggled all her life so I could be something.

ROBERTA. What? A sex maniac?

REED. I can't be with her tonight—there's no way. And it just kills me to think of her being all alone.

ROBERTA. (*Puts phone down.*) Why isn't your father with her?

REED. He was killed in Korea. Red Cross.

ROBERTA. That makes you younger than I thought.

REED. Oh, merciful God—if I lose her! (*Sobs.*)

ROBERTA. (*Sits beside him.*) Is it her heart?

REED. She wouldn't tell me. She didn't want to worry me. Isn't that wonderful?

ROBERTA. I'm sorry I misunderstood what you were going through.

REED. Oh, thank you, Roberta. (*Hugs her.*) You've been such a help. I can never repay your kindness. You're *so* dear. So sweet. You even smell like my mother.

ROBERTA. She wears "Lust"?

REED. I mean clean—fresh—morning dew—night rain—spring flowers. (*Kisses her hand.*) "And all the perfumes of Arabia will not sweeten this little hand."

ROBERTA. Shakespeare. Macbeth.

REED. Now, how did you know *that?*

ROBERTA. I played the witch once.

REED. You're *such* good company, Roberta. Stay with me. Just an hour or two.

ROBERTA. I can't—

REED. Help me over this traumatic hurdle.

ROBERTA. I've got a three o'clock class in pottery.

REED. Then come back. I need someone to spend this night with me — to share this vigil.

ROBERTA. Spend the *night?*

REED. We'll just sit up and talk.

ROBERTA. About Molière — or your mother?

REED. I don't trust myself alone tonight. Do you know when I was little and she had her hysterectomy, I tried to commit suicide?

ROBERTA. Well, I'll tell you what I *will* do. I'll come back to cook your dinner for you.

REED. You will? Really. Oh, bless you — bless you.

ROBERTA. Shall I bring anything?

REED. Your toothbrush. (*Grins.*)

ROBERTA. That's no way to talk on Mother's Day.

REED. But you'll be back? Seven o'clock?

ROBERTA. Scout's honor. (*Goes to door.*)

REED. You're sure you can't stay *now?*

ROBERTA. No. If I do, I'll be sorry.

REED. Afraid?

ROBERTA. Afraid you wouldn't finish my Molière. (*She goes out. He bounces back to the card table to resume work. He has no sooner started than the door chimes sound.*)

REED. Oh, shit! (*Yells.*) Come on — come in! (*Angie Pepperdine, another attractive student, a little more formally attired, enters with a manuscript.*)

ANGIE. Are you busy, Professor Dolan?

REED. Well, not *too* busy.

ANGIE. Do you remember me?

REED. You're not by any chance someone named Vanessa, are you?

ANGIE. No, Angie. I'm the one that threw up at auditions yesterday.

REED. Oh, yes. I remember. Feeling better?

ANGIE. Lots. That's why I'm here. I wonder if you'd let me read again for that part in *Scandal Point.*

REED. Which part was that?

ANGIE. The prostitute.

REED. Well, young lady — have you had any experience — as an *actress?*

ANGIE. Very little — as an *actress*. I was only in one play before. That was *Alice in Wonderland*.

REED. As Alice?

ANGIE. No — the rabbit.

REED. Good. I'll call you Bunny. (*He laughs with disarming cameraderie.*) Sit down, dear.

ANGIE. Thank you. When I got out of the shower this morning, I looked in the mirror and I said Angie Pepperdine, you can play that prostitute better than Bernadine Durdle — if Professor Dolan will just give you another chance to read.

REED. Good. I like your attitude. But I wonder, dear, if you're quite old enough to play an experienced prostitute? (*Sits facing her.*)

ANGIE. But experience doesn't depend on age, does it? Did you know a girl in Peru had a baby at nine?

REED. Really? Well, it's a hot climate. Are you from the South?

ANGIE. Vermont. On the other hand, my Aunt Prudy is ninety and still a virgin.

REED. Ah — but does she want to play a prostitute.

ANGIE. Do you think I look too young? If I were that girl from Peru, I could be a grandmother by now.

REED. How lucky you're from Vermont.

ANGIE. Do you think I'm physically wrong?

REED. No — no — no. I'd say physically you're quite adequate. How old *are* you — just as a matter of record.

ANGIE. Emotionally — intellectually or chronologically?

REED. Well, when one votes, one is *not* asked their *intellectual* age.

ANGIE. I'm older than I look. I'm nineteen.

REED. Ah — not yet a woman — not still a child.

ANGIE. Oh, do you write poetry? I do.

REED. I'm not that gifted. Now, before we start, can I offer you a drink?

ANGIE. No. I'm still nervous. I wouldn't want to throw up on you.

REED. Relax, dear. Just place yourself in my hands. I see you brought your script. I'll sit beside you and read over your shoulder. (*Sits beside her on sofa.*)

ANGIE. I can't tell you how much I appreciate this, Professor Dolan.

REED. We're not in the classroom, Angie, so we can dispense with protocol. My name is "Reed."

ANGIE. Oh, I couldn't call you "Reed," sir.

REED. Now, why not?

ANGIE. That's the name of my dog.

REED. I promise not to bite. (*Laughs with intimate humor.*)

ANGIE. (*Opens her script.*) If it's all right with you, I'll read the big speech where she tells off the Senator.

REED. Whatever puts you at ease, dear.

ANGIE. (*Puts glasses on.*) I have to wear glasses to read but I won't when I learn the part. I don't think prostitutes wear glasses.

REED. Not professionally.

ANGIE. Well, here goes. (*Reads.*) "You may be a senator, Senator, and I am only a whore who has sold her body. But *you* have sold your soul. You have betrayed your country while I have only betrayed myself. What I have done, I have done thru need. What you have done you've done thru greed. No man of honor sells his soul solely for success. I have been your mistress but you have not mastered me. You took me from the streets and to the streets I now return. No — it is futile to argue for futility reapeth a barren harvest. Bear that in mind in your lonely hours alone. Goodbye, sir." (*She looks up.*) Eek!

REED. That's beautiful!

ANGIE. It's pretty purple, isn't it? Who wrote this tripe — Albee?

REED. I mean your conviction — your vocal quality — the suggestion of the libidinous.

ANGIE. How'd you happen to pick *this* play, sir? *Reed.*

REED. It's a classic in Spain.

ANGIE. Oh, well, maybe it loses something in translation. Still, I'd like to play it. Every girl wants to play a prostitute once — like being blonde.

REED. (*Leans toward her.*) What is that *delightful* perfume you're wearing?

ANGIE. I'm sorry you asked.

REED. Why?

15

ANGIE. It's got a revolting name. (*Continues to look for next speech.*)

REED. "Lust"?

ANGIE. Is that a perfume?

REED. Sometimes.

ANGIE. I thought it was a sport. (*Laughs.*)

REED. Sometimes. What's yours called?

ANGIE. I don't know you well enough to say it.

REED. That's not my fault. What is it?

ANGIE. Alright—you asked. It's called "Morning Yen." Isn't that awful?

REED. Depends on the company.

ANGIE. It belongs to my roommate, Roberta Gutman. I think she gets her perfumes from a sex catalogue. She's one of your students, too.

REED. I can't quite place her. But she must smell very good.

ANGIE. (*Finds place in script.*) Shall I go on?

REED. (*Moves closer.*) Please. I want to get a better concept of your projection.

ANGIE. (*Flips pages.*) This is where the judge sentences her for shooting the Senator. She should have shot the playwright.

REED. You're wrong, honey. This play is just obscure enough to seem profound. That's why I chose it.

ANGIE. Well, for what it's worth. (*Reads.*) "Your Honor, if I may call you that—you have condemned me to prison but—I have lived in prison all my life. The prison of use and abuse—the prison of apprehension and convention—the prison of dominion and opinion—the prison of affection and rejection—and the prison of strife and life itself. So prison is not punishment for this deed. I have no regrets. No remorse. I have been of service to many men. And now in ridding our nation of a man who betrayed it, I have performed a patriotic service to my country, myself and my God." (*Stops.*) My God—that stinks.

REED. It's art, dear. In college theater we try to avoid the taint of commercialism.

ANGIE. Shall I wade on?

REED. No need. You've convinced me you'd make a very good prostitute.

16

ANGIE. You mean you'll let *me* play the part instead of Bernadine Durdle?

REED. I'd have cast you yesterday if you hadn't thrown up.

ANGIE. Oh, Professor Dolan. (*Grabs him and kisses him.*) Oh, I
shouldn't have done that.

REED. No — you shouldn't have. There is an old Chinese prov-
erb — "Never wake a sleeping tiger." (*He grabs her and she responds with an unexpected intensity that overwhelms Reed. They writhe
entwined like mating milk snakes. Reed finally disengages for the benefit
of his lungs.*) Well, I certainly didn't expect *this* response to a
Spanish play.

ANGIE. You should have. Oh, Professor Dolan — *Reed* — I've
been in love with you since the first day I walked into Restora-
tion Comedy II.

REED. You have? But I never suspected.

ANGIE. Of course not. You were always so forbidding — so
unattainable — so academic. I dream about you. I write poetry
about you. Kiss me again. (*He kisses her.*)

REED. Control yourself, child. We mustn't shoot a rabbit with
a cannon.

ANGIE. (*Clings to him.*) A year ago when I came into class you
said, "Good morning." I almost died. Kiss me again. (*He does.*)

REED. Well, I must say I certainly didn't expect *this* tempestu-
ous reaction.

ANGIE. Of course not. You don't know how "steamy" you are.
How "thermal."

REED. (*Shrugs modestly.*) Well —

ANGIE. Kiss me. (*He does.*) I love you. I love you. I love you.
Kiss me again.

REED. Angie — you're dissipating your energy. One gets better
mileage with less speed.

ANGIE. Why do you think I threw up? You touched me at
auditions.

REED. Well, let's hope in the future it isn't habitual.

ANGIE. And all those other nasty girls trying to get your attention. Kiss me. (*He does.*)

REED. Would you mind being just a little less ardent, dear?

ANGIE. Why?

REED. You're getting lipstick on my shirt.

ANGIE. Take it off.

REED. Angie—give me a moment to recover from shock.

ANGIE. Can I move in with you?

REED. Well, not right away, dear. You see I don't have *tenure.* But we'll arrange something tentative.

ANGIE. When? Tonight? I'll cook dinner for you.

REED. No—not tonight. My sister is coming at seven.

ANGIE. Breakfast?

REED. She's staying over. But how about this weekend? Have you ever been to Lake Hocapocapoo?

ANGIE. Isn't that in Utah?

REED. (*Shakes his head.*) Only an hour away. I've a cabin up there. We could sneak off right after "Improvisation One" and no one would know, except you and I and the zenith moon.

ANGIE. Oh, Reed—to be *alone* with *you!* Kiss me. (*He does.*) I've got a wig. I'll wear it to protect your reputation. Kiss me. (*He does.*) It's red, tho. Does that matter?

REED. It's your *reputation* I'm thinking of, dear. On second thought—why wait till the weekend to consolidate our common interests. Why not take advantage of our present propinquity.

ANGIE. Oh, Reed—don't! My stomach is turning over.

REED. Well, why don't you go into the bathroom and take a Bromo. And a warm shower might calm you a little. (*She hugs him. The door chimes are heard.*) Oh, shit. (*He goes to open the door. Ingrid Novotny, a rather voluptuous student in a tight, revealing sweater, enters.*)

INGRID. Oh. Am I interrupting you?

REED. No, I was just reading this young lady for a role she'd like to play. Are you Vanessa?

INGRID. No. Ingrid, Ingrid Novotny. I'm taking your "Medieval Passion Plays" course.

REED. Oh yes, Ingrid. I remember you now. Well, what can I do for you, Ingrid?

INGRID. Well, I did want to talk to you about my paper—if you could spare the time.

REED. Could you come back in about an hour? Make it two.

INGRID. No—actually, I can't, I'm baby-sitting.

ANGIE. (*Rises.*) Look, it's all right, Professor Dolan. You have your duty here. I'll read for you again this weekend. Besides, I

18

just remembered I have to go anyway. I haven't phoned my mother, and it's Mother's Day.

INGRID. (*To Angie.*) Oh, don't let me intrude on *your* time. I could sit here and wait until you're thru.

ANGIE. Thank you but I get nervous if anybody is watching.

REED. She throws up.

INGRID. Well, I could come back—say around seven?

REED. No—no, I'll be busy at seven. I'm expecting my sister at seven.

ANGIE. It's quite all right, Professor. I think we made progress this session. (*Gathers up her papers.*) Thank you for your time. It was very productive. (*At door.*) It would really be futile to start the next act now. As the man said—"Futility reapeth a barren harvest." Bye. (*She goes out.*)

REED. Now, Miss Novotny. Incidentally, what is "Novotny"?

INGRID. My name.

REED. I mean the ethnic genesis. Is it Scandinavian?

INGRID. Polish.

REED. No!

INGRID. Why?

REED. Well, I'm Polish, too. We start with a common bond.

INGRID. But Dolan isn't Polish. It's Celtic, isn't it?

REED. It used to be Dolansky. (*Offers his hand.*) Shake hands. One Pole to another. Sit down, dear. What can I do for you?

INGRID. (*Sits.*) Save my life.

REED. And just how do I do that?

INGRID. Have you graded my paper yet?

REED. What was your subject?

INGRID. "Pornography in Greek Drama."

REED. No, but it's a paper I look forward to, dear.

INGRID. Well, the reason I'm here is, last year I barely got by on my grades. This year, if I get one "A" in *anything,* my father promised he'd give me a Honda.

REED. Why did you pick a Honda?

INGRID. I didn't. He's the distributor.

REED. Well, since I haven't read your paper, I haven't graded it yet.

INGRID. You won't have to.

REED. I don't understand.

INGRID. I'm here to trade favors.

REED. I don't understand.

INGRID. It's simple. You give me an "A" in "Greek Pornography in Drama" and I'll give you a night in this apartment that'll eclipse anything any Greek ever saw anytime, anywhere in Greece.

REED. I don't understand.

INGRID. Tit for tat — if you'll pardon my vulgarity.

REED. I think I understand.

INGRID. Well, what do you say, Professor?

REED. Allow me to say that this is the most unheard of thing I've ever heard of.

INGRID. I promise you, I'll deserve the "A" for aptitude.

REED. Whatever made you think I would consent to such a degrading scholastic exchange.

INGRID. Oh, word gets around.

REED. And what does that innuendo imply?

INGRID. Oh, I've several girlfriends who've told me about your cabin up at Lake Hocapocapoo. By the way — what does Hocapocapoo mean? Is it Indian for "Hot Pillow"?

REED. I don't listen to vicious gossip.

INGRID. I do. Sometimes it pays off. Is it a deal?

REED. Of course not. Why, if I ever stooped to such a tawdry exchange of favors, it would cause a public scandal. My father is a senator.

INGRID. Oh, *I'd* never tell. I'll swear that on a Bible.

REED. Such an oath would be sacrilegious.

INGRID. You mean you won't negotiate?

REED. Miss Novotny, I am a person of probity. I believe it to be my duty as a teacher to adhere to the highest standards — both academic and morally. And you shock me by denigrating both. No man of honor would sell his soul solely for success.

INGRID. Well, do you believe in compromise?

REED. On occasion.

INGRID. Then let's compromise. I'll take a "B" minus. That's good for a motorbike.

REED. Miss Novotny — the only relationship between a teacher and a student should be on the highest intellectual level. You are making Socrates turn over in his grave.

INGRID. One less witness.

REED. Why, if the slightest hint of even this *conversation* reached unsympathetic ears, I'd lose my tenure, particularly if you were not of voting age.

INGRID. I'm safely past that. Also the age of discretion.

REED. Did you really think I'd agree to exchanging my scholastic standards for a fleeting moment of carnal pleasure? I'm appalled.

INGRID. Yes—I really did. (*Rises.*) But I guess I was wrong. Well, I'll go back to the dorm and put a Band-aid on my pride. (*Starts for door.*) At least we won't upset Socrates.

REED. (*Lets her get to the door.*) However—since the Honda is so important to you—

INGRID. (*Races back to him.*) Oh, Professor—you mean you will!

REED. Well, I don't like to be petty. And although I do have a heavy schedule, if we bypass the preliminaries, we just might have time to resolve your dilemma.

INGRID. Lock the door.

REED. But remember—no word must ever get out about this reciprocal transaction.

INGRID. My ethics are above question.

REED. And keep in mind that the world's best-kept secret is an egg—until it's broken.

INGRID. Where do we rendezvous?

REED. (*Points to bedroom.*) I'll fix drinks and join you. Don't start without me.

INGRID. (*Goes to door and stops.*) Oh, there's something you ought to know about me first. I have an appendectomy scar. (*Exits.*)

REED. (*Shrugs.*) How do I get into these things. I must be a pussy cat—I always fall on my feet. (*Goes to bar. As he is fixing drinks, the door chimes make him jump, dropping ice cubes.*) Oh, shit! (*He crosses to open door. Hercules Homer Hunter, a florid man of impressive weight, enters and stands before him.*)

HUNTER. Professor Dolan?

REED. That's right.

HUNTER. May I come in?

REED. Well, I'm rather busy at the moment.

HUNTER. I'll just take a minute. (*Pushes past him.*) I'm Hercules Homer Hunter. (*Offers his hand. Reed winces at the pressure of his grip.*) Does that name mean anything to you?

REED. Just that it's alliterative.

HUNTER. I'm Zenobia's father.

REED. Zenobia?

HUNTER. Your fiancee's father.

REED. I'm afraid there's some mistake, Mister Hunter. I don't know any Zenobia—except historically. And I have no fiancee.

HUNTER. Oh, you don't have to be sly with me, son. I know she promised you not to tell anyone until you got this tenure of office. But I'm her father.

REED. Mr. Hercules Homer Hunter—I teach Homer incidentally—I have two hundred drama majors in my classes. If there was a Zenobia, I'd know. Particularly since she comes at the end of the alphabet.

HUNTER. Is there another Professor Dolan?

REED. No, I'm afraid that after me, God broke the mold. (*Laughs affably.*)

HUNTER. But she wrote saying she was engaged to you.

REED. That couldn't be possible. I'm already married.

HUNTER. Maybe your wife could explain. Is she here?

REED. No. Unfortunately, she's still in a private mental hospital. She had a breakdown after we lost our little girl.

HUNTER. Sorry about that, son. Well, my little girl must have meant some other teacher. She'd written us about *you* and I assumed you was he.

REED. Well, you're wrong, sir—specifically and grammatically.

HUNTER. (*Starts toward door.*) I guess I better find her and find out just who she *did* mean. (*Stops.*) Wait a minute. Zenobia sent me a snapshot of her and him.

REED. Well, I have the misfortune to look like nearly everybody.

HUNTER. (*Takes out picture.*) There. It isn't very clear and he's got on dark glasses but it certainly looks like *you.*

REED. (*Slumps down.*) But I'm much shorter than that.

HUNTER. You didn't take her on a Wild Flower tour last Mother's Day at a place called Lake Hocapocapoo?

REED. That's in Utah, isn't it?

HUNTER. Well, there's something mighty wrong here. In her

letter she says she can't come home this Mother's Day because she's going up to this lake to meet your parents.

REED. Well, that proves she's not referring to me. I have no parents. Obviously, Mr. Hunter, your daughter is using me as a scapegoat for some student she's having an affair with. I don't know your daughter. I never have heard of Hocapocapoo. If you like, I'll swear that on a Bible. Wait. (*Goes up to desk and picks up a book.*) Maybe this will convince you. (*He lifts his hand.*) I swear on this Holy Bible that I have never heard of anyone named Zenobia — except historically.

HUNTER. Or Hocapocapoo?

REED. Or Hocapocapoo.

HUNTER. Well, I guess that's that. I apologize for bothering you, son.

REED. Not at all. As the Bible says, "It is human to err." Now, if you'll excuse me, I have a date with the Dean.

HUNTER. (*Comes up to offer hand.*) And no hard feelings. (*They shake hands. Reed winces. Hunter looks down. He picks up the "Bible."*) That's not the Bible! (*Reads.*) It's the Boston Cookbook.

REED. Well, what do you know! I didn't have my glasses. Well, it is the Bible in Boston. Now where is my King James Version? (*Starts looking around. Ingrid comes out practically nude.*)

INGRID. Reed — how long are you — (*She stops and tries to cover herself with a sofa pillow.*)

REED. (*To Hunter.*) Oh, this is my kid sister, Ingrid. She's just changing to go back to her school. (*To Ingrid.*) You better hurry, dear. Mother will be worried.

HUNTER. I thought you didn't have any parents.

REED. She goes to a convent. I was referring to the Mother Superior. (*To Ingrid.*) You'll have to leave right away, dear. I have a sudden date with the Dean. (*Ingrid dashes back into the bedroom.*)

HUNTER. You're acting mighty peculiar, boy. Look here, Professor — have you got my little girl in trouble?

REED. What do you mean — "in trouble"?

HUNTER. You know damn well what I mean.

REED. Sir, in the academic world, we like to be specific. There is financial trouble, family trouble, tax trouble, kidney trouble —

HUNTER. Well, I don't mean kidney trouble. But you're getting warm.

REED. By any chance—do you mean impregnated?

HUNTER. That's exactly what I mean—knocked up.

REED. (*Winces.*) Sir, I abhor that expression. I'm not only offended by its grammatical incongruity but also its bromidic vulgarity.

HUNTER. Cut the shit, son. In Texas, we don't mince words. But we sure as hell mince those mongrels that knock up our daughters.

REED. Would you like to know *why* that's an impossible allegation?

HUNTER. This better be good.

REED. I happen to be sterile.

HUNTER. That's good. But not good enough.

REED. Well, it happens to be true. During the war, I had the misfortune to fall on a grenade. My genitalia were utterly destroyed. That's why your suspicions have no validity.

HUNTER. You mean you're—you're what we call in Texas—a steer?

REED. Well, the comparison isn't flattering but it does approximate my physiological shortcoming.

HUNTER. You telling me you're a eunuch?

REED. You could say that—in the oriental sense.

HUNTER. Show me.

REED. Oh come now, Mr. Hunter. Surely you don't intend to subject me to *that* indignity.

HUNTER. I sure do. In Texas I've castrated pigs. I know what it looks like.

REED. If you don't mind my saying so I resent being placed in the same category.

HUNTER. Quit stalling, man. Show me.

REED. (*Backing up.*) Are all Texans as suspicious as you?

HUNTER. That's why we're rich. Down in God's Country we lay our cards on the table.

REED. That's just the point. I've nothing to lay on the table.

HUNTER. You want me to take your pants off?

REED. I tell you what I'll do. I'll get you a statement from my doctor.

HUNTER. Better yet—get him on the phone.

REED. He's on vacation. (*At this point, Ingrid comes out of the bedroom fully dressed.*)

24

INGRID. Well, I always say life is complicated and sometimes I get tired saying it. (*Crosses to entrance door.*)

REED. I'd drive you to the bus station, dear, but I've got a date with the Dean. Take care.

INGRID. (*At door.*) Well, there goes my Honda. (*Exits.*)

REED. Sweet girl. She's thinking of becoming a nun. Now, if you'll excuse me, the Dean is waiting. One of our students tried to commit suicide.

HUNTER. Well, you better consider that option yourself if I find out you've been lying to me.

REED. I don't like to seem immodest, sir, but my reputation here precludes such an assumption. However, if I can be of any assistance — I'm chairman of the advisory committee.

HUNTER. (*Goes to door.*) And if my *Zenobia's* been lying to *me,* I'm going to kick her ass all the way back to Dallas.

REED. Surely that's rather extreme, Mr. Hunter. Wouldn't Houston be far enough?

HUNTER. And *yours* to Corpus Christi. (*He slams out. Reed leans against the door and looks heavenward.*)

REED. Oh, Lord — why *me?* I live right. (*He dashes for the phone and dials. He puts the phone down and quickly splashes himself a drink. He dashes back to the phone to wait.*) Hello! Zenobia? Did you know your father's here? Well, he is. Why the hell did you write him we were engaged. No! I want to know right *now!* I've got to protect my family's reputation — my uncle is a Catholic bishop. You better explain in a hurry because he's on his way over to kick your little ass all the way to Neiman-Marcus. Zenobia? *Hello! Hello!* (*He clicks the receiver and then hangs up angrily.*) That's gratitude! You predatory little Jezebel. (*Gulps his drink.*) This isn't one of my better days. (*The door chimes are heard. He groans.*) Oh, shit! (*Yells.*) Come in! (*Vanessa Jacobs, a chic, assured and otherwise well assembled woman of about thirty, enters. She stands for a moment, smiling at him.*) Yes?

VANESSA. Is that all — yes?

REED. Oh, God — you're not *Mrs.* Hercules Homer Hunter, are you!

VANESSA. My married name is Jacobs. You really don't remember me, do you?

REED. Well, I suffer sometimes from memory lapses. A childhood accident.

VANESSA. (*Laughs.*) And to think you once told me you'd *never* forget me.

REED. I did? (*Smiles disarmingly.*) Well, blame that *horse* that threw me, Mrs. Jacobs, not me.

VANESSA. I'm Vanessa, Reed.

REED. Vanessa. Oh, yes—you phoned this morning and then hung up.

VANESSA. We were disconnected. And then, my plane was announced.

REED. Vanessa? That doesn't ring a bell.

VANESSA. It *should* ring a gong. You don't remember Holy Week and Lake Hocapocapoo? Ten years ago?

REED. Ten years ago? I was in Viet Nam.

VANESSA. You were *here*. It was your first year here as a teacher. I was a freshman, Vanessa Miller.

REED. Vanessa Miller! Little Vannie? (*Takes her hand warmly.*) Why, you've grown into a *beautiful* woman. No wonder I didn't know you.

VANESSA. Well, *you* certainly haven't changed.

REED. Sit down and tell me all about yourself, Vannie. Would you like a drink?

VANESSA. (*Shakes her head.*) Do you remember the first drink I ever had was with you?

REED. Oh, no—not me. I wouldn't give a drink to a *freshman*.

VANESSA. (*Sits.*) Well, I remember. And *I* didn't fall off a horse.

REED. (*Sits beside her.*) So you're married. Where's your husband?

VANESSA. Dead. (*Powders her nose.*)

REED. Oh, I'm so sorry. (*Pats her shoulder.*)

VANESSA. One adjusts. Time creeps on—and one stands up again.

REED. Well, what brings you to this neck of the woods?

VANESSA. Nostalgia. And a duty to my husband.

REED. Well, I'm flattered that you looked me up. (*Takes her hands.*)

VANESSA. Even tho' you'd forgotten Hocapocapoo?

REED. I remember perfectly, now. We got up there at night. There was a canoe and a zenith moon.

VANESSA. It was raining. And you built a fire in the cabin.

26

REED. I did?

VANESSA. Yes. Under me.

REED. (*Releases her hands and straightens up warily.*) How long are you going to be around in our exalted halls of learning?

VANESSA. That depends. So you're still a bachelor?

REED. How'd you know that?

VANESSA. I asked one of your students.

REED. Oh? I wasn't aware they knew anything of my personal life.

VANESSA. Her father sold me a car. A Honda.

REED. I wonder who that can be? I've so many students now, I can't keep track of them.

VANESSA. And far be it from me to challenge your track record.

REED. Now, Vannie, do you think that's a fair thing to say? I've matured since those innocent days *you* led me astray.

VANESSA. I'll let that pass and get to the reason I came here. You see I made a promise to my husband that involves *you*.

REED. Me. Me?

VANESSA. You see, I have a son.

REED. Congratulations!

VANESSA. Named Reed.

REED. (*Pauses.*) You—you named him after *me?*

VANESSA. Don't you think it's a good Christian name?

REED. Oh, yes—but I don't deserve an honor like that—not me.

VANESSA. Oh, but *you do*. I always say a boy should be named after his father.

REED. (*Gives a silly, absurd, uncomfortable laugh.*) You mean—I mean—you think I'm his father?

VANESSA. I know you are.

REED. But that's impossible. I'm sterile. Unfortunately I fell on a grenade in Vietnam.

VANESSA. You fell on me first, unfortunately.

REED. Well. Well, if you thought *I* was the father, why didn't you tell me?

VANESSA. I loved you. I didn't want to burden you. You had a crippled mother to support.

REED. Oh. Well, I still think you might have told me. You owed me that courtesy as a co-operative contributor.

VANESSA. No. But I did tell a nice man who loved me and

27

married me anyhow. And he made me promise that if anything ever happened to him and the boy didn't have a father—I should bring him to you.

REED. Me?

VANESSA. You.

REED. What for?

VANESSA. You're his father. You have a son. Isn't that natural?

REED. Well, it *would* be natural if you presented me with a son at nine pounds—but not nine years. That's not a natural birth, Vanessa.

VANESSA. Don't you want to know something about him?

REED. Sure. What does he weigh?

VANESSA. Haven't you any paternal interest in seeing him?

REED. Of course. Did you bring a picture?

VANESSA. I did better than that. I brought *him.*

REED. You've got to be kidding.

VANESSA. Well, the *kid's* here. (*Rises and opens the hall door.*) Reed, come in and meet your father. (*Reed stands apprehensively. A nine-year-old boy steps in and after a brief hesitation, makes for Reed with arms outstretched.*)

BOY. Daddy! (*He throws his arms around Reed's legs and slides down to the floor, still clinging tenaciously.*)

REED. Get him off of me! Get him off of me! (*He backs up, trying to shake the boy off as one would a friendly puppy.*)

CURTAIN

ACT II

PLACE: *The same.*

TIME: *A few hours later.*

AT RISE: *Vanessa has taken off her jacket and sits on the sofa sipping a drink. The boy is curled up asleep beside her.*
Reed is pacing around the room nervously, chain smoking. He pauses to glare with wary distaste at the sleeping boy.

REED. (*Stops beside Vanessa.*) Look—don't think I don't appreciate what you've spared me, Vannie, but *I* can't raise a kid, that's a woman's job.

VANESSA. He needs the influence of a father.

REED. That's a terrible responsibility you're asking me to assume. It's like asking me to be Pope.

VANESSA. If you were Pope, I wouldn't ask you.

REED. I'd make a lousy father and you know it. I didn't tell you but I've become alcoholic. (*He extends a trembling hand for proof.*)

VANESSA. A son will sober you.

REED. Now, Vanessa, sweetie, be sensible, dear. Something else I haven't told you. Lately, I've begun to doubt my masculinity—to wonder if I'm not basically a latent homosexual. I've been going to a faggot analyst to find out.

VANESSA. That's a good idea. One should always be cocksure.

REED. And something else you didn't know. I've never forgotten you. Not a day has passed that I haven't thought of you. I think you owe me a little compensation? Take the kid and go someplace.

VANESSA. Where? Lake Hocapocapoo?

REED. I know you won't believe this but after I lost you I became a miserable misanthrope. And to show you how desperate I was, I even considered becoming a Jesuit.

VANESSA. God help the nuns.

29

REED. Look, sweetie — if it's a question of money, I'll take on a few extra students for private tutoring.

VANESSA. When did you ever stop?

REED. I'll be glad to contribute to child support — my share — and also to support him spiritually. In good faith. In absentia.

VANESSA. No need. He's been baptized, subsidized and circumcised.

REED. Hey! I've got a *good* constructive idea! What about a nice military school?

VANESSA. (*Rises.*) Reed — I don't want to have to haul you into court. I'd like to settle this between us *now*. *You're* to keep him for six months and *I'll* keep him for six months.

REED. Six months! Vanessa, you shock me. What sort of a mother are you to abandon your own son for six months?

VANESSA. What sort of father are you?

REED. A perfectly normal one. The male animal doesn't always feel protective about his accidental progeny. Some animals even eat their offspring. *Lions* do.

VANESSA. And chimpanzees. Which are you?

REED. Who'd look after him? I don't know how to change diapers.

VANESSA. He's past that. You'd only have to wipe his nose.

REED. (*Pushes her back on the sofa.*) Baby, it's not that I don't want to face my responsibilities. I'm thinking primarily of the kid. As a teacher here, I'll be forced to neglect him and he'd grow up neurotic — retarded. You see, I consider the dissemination of knowledge a holy mandate for me. Like St. Paul.

VANESSA. I had a beloved grandmother who was a saint. And she said something wonderful once that applies to you.

REED. (*Flattered.*) Really? What?

VANESSA. Once a shit, always a shit. And someday, sonny, you're going to trip over your duplicity and fall *"flat on your face."*

REED. What really disappoints me, Vanessa, is to find you vindictive. I always thought of you as a Madonna.

VANESSA. Thanks, dear, but mine was *not* an immaculate conception.

REED. (*Haughtily.*) I consider that remark sacrilegious. You offend me as a decent Catholic who almost became a Jesuit because of you.

VANESSA. I'm surprised you didn't pick the Trappist order of monks. They combine *veracity* with celibacy.

REED. Oh. So you don't believe me. Well, I just happen to have the Jesuit vow right here. (*He picks up the Molière script.*) Are you familiar with Latin?

VANESSA. Just the phrase—"In God we trust." No others.

REED. Well, this is the sacred vow I was about to take as a Jesuit. (*He reads the Molière appointment.*) Deo teste meo, ut Johannus Baptistus Poquelinis hinc ad munus suppelectilis regalis instruendae designaretur de manu ipsa ego Ludivicus tredecimus, rex Galliae decrevi. (*He looks up smugly.*) Would you care to have me translate that for you? (*He puts it safely in a drawer.*)

VANESSA. Not particularly.

REED. Well, it says this: "God—God bear witness that I, Reed Dolan, do herewith accept the sacred Jesuit vows of poverty, self-denial and celibacy in the name of the Father, the Son and the Holy Ghost."

VANESSA. You'd never have made Pope.

REED. (*Sinks on his knees beside her.*) Oh, Vanessa, cherub—how can I convince you that my real dedication is here—as a layman?

VANESSA. You don't have to convince me. I *know* from experience. (*She brushes the boy's hair back from his forehead.*)

REED. (*Jumps up.*) Don't wake him! (*The boy sits up.*) Now see what you've done. He'll be at my legs again. (*He gets behind a chair.*)

BOY. (*Yawns.*) I'm hungry.

REED. My God . . . he's got teeth like a baby gorilla.

BOY. I want a banana.

REED. And the same appetite.

VANESSA. Do you happen to have a banana?

REED. What would I be doing with a banana? I've never entertained a monkey here. Until now.

VANESSA. Do you have any milk?

REED. I don't keep a cat either. But I'm going to need milk mighty soon. You're giving me an ulcer.

VANESSA. Any crackers?

REED. You don't see a parrot, do you?

VANESSA. Well, you must have *something* nourishing here.

REED. I do. Beer—gin—vodka—rum. You *see,* he'd end up a nine-year-old alcoholic.

VANESSA. More likely a nine-year-old sex maniac.

BOY. (*Shouts.*) *I'm hungry!*

REED. All right! All right! I'll take some cheese out of a trap.

BOY. I'm no rat. I don't want any of your dirty old rat cheese.

REED. (*To Vanessa.*) You hear that kind of disrespect? Six months of that and I'd kill him. Do *you* want to be guilty of making me a murderer?

BOY. No, you wouldn't.

REED. Oh, no? And what makes you think I wouldn't?

BOY. I'd kill you first.

REED. There! There! You expect me to live with a junior member of the Mafia and keep my sanity? Vanessa, I flatly refuse to assume *your* responsibilities.

VANESSA. (*Rises.*) Very well—I'll see you in court.

REED. Now, wait a minute, sweetheart. Let's talk this over sensibly. You're getting all upset. Sit down, pet.

BOY. *I want a banana.*

REED. Oh, shut up!

BOY. Make me.

VANESSA. Now, *stop* this. You're both getting off to a bad start. (*Turns to boy.*) Reedie Beadie, apologize.

REED. Reedie *Beadie!*

VANESSA. It's his pet name.

REED. Sounds like a detergent for toilets.

VANESSA. Reedie Beadie, apologize to your father.

BOY. No. Make him apologize to me. He called me a dirty name.

REED. A detergent isn't dirty.

BOY. Well, a toilet is.

VANESSA. He's right. Reed, apologize to your son for demeaning him.

REED. Me? To *it?*

VANESSA. Adults should set a good example.

BOY. Yea. He called me an "it."

VANESSA. Reed, you're creating a very bad impression on the boy. Show some magnanimity.

REED. Alright! Alright! (*Bows to boy.*) Would you be so gracious as to accept my profound apologies for calling you a detergent?

BOY. And an "it."

REED. *And* an "it"!

BOY. I'll think about it.

REED. That's very gracious of you.

VANESSA. Reed, you're not trying. He's your son. Talk to him. Express an interest in him. You'll find it very rewarding.

REED. All right. Well, Reedie Beadie — what do you want to be when you grow up?

BOY. A man. What do you want to be?

REED. (*Storms away.*) Did you hear that! He's already a nine-year-old half-ass smart-ass.

VANESSA. (*Takes boy by the shoulder.*) And, baby — you're showing the bad side of your nature that you inherited from your father. Now, I want you to show the good side of your nature that you inherited from *me.* Show him how sweet and affectionate you really are. Go put your arms around him and give him a big kiss — for *me.*

REED. That's all right. No need to be emotionally excessive. It only provokes premature puberty.

VANESSA. You should know. (*To boy.*) Go ahead, baby. Please.

BOY. If it's for you, why don't *you* do it?

VANESSA. He's not my father — he's yours. Go ahead. Kiss him. (*The boy crosses to Reed, standing behind a chair. He climbs up on the chair and puts his arms around Reed's neck and kisses him on the cheek. Reed yells.*)

REED. He bit me!

VANESSA. Reed! Did you bite your father!

BOY. He pinched me.

REED. I did not! I held onto his arms so he wouldn't fall, the little bastard.

VANESSA. That may be true but it won't help to remind him. Sit down, Reedie Beadie. Reed, tell your son you're sorry.

REED. (*To boy.*) All right — all right — I'm sorry. What more do you want?

BOY. A banana.

REED. Vanessa, what else does it take to convince you this is a totally intolerable situation. I can't live with a baby cobra. Put him in a seminary — a correction home — a reliable kennels. (*The door opens and Zenobia, a very pretty girl, very distraught, looks in, peering into the hall. She closes the door slowly and turns around.*)

ZENOBIA. Oh! I thought you'd be alone.

REED. Oh, hello, Zenobia. (*To Vanessa.*) Vanessa, this is one of my very promising students in "Improvisation Two." Zenobia — Hunter, isn't it? Sorry, but I have a mental block about names.

ZENOBIA. Yes — "Hunter" as in "Safari." Could I see you for a moment, Professor Dolan? Alone?

REED. Oh, that's all right. My guests were just leaving. (*To Vanessa.*) Do you have a car — or shall I call a taxi for you, Mrs. Jacobs.

VANESSA. Oh, no. I've hours to spare. We'll wait in your bedroom. I'll nurse him. (*Rises.*)

REED. I'm afraid you'll find my room too unpleasant — it's just been painted.

VANESSA. Oh, I won't mind the odor — *I* have a *nasal* block. Come Reedie Beadie, I'll read to you about the big bad wolf. (*Goes to bedroom door and takes boy inside.*)

ZENOBIA. Who is she?

REED. An old schoolmate of my oldest sister. She dropped in to show me her son. What the hell are *you* doing here!

ZENOBIA. I came to warn you about Dad.

REED. You're too late.

ZENOBIA. He has a terrible temper. He's very unreasonable.

REED. What else is new?

ZENOBIA. And a gun.

REED. A gun! Well, he wouldn't be that unreasonable, would he?

ZENOBIA. He killed a low-down thieving coyote once in Texas with his bare hands.

REED. He killed a man!

ZENOBIA. No — a coyote.

REED. Why in the name of God did you write him that you were engaged to me?

ZENOBIA. I wanted to impress him. They wanted me to fly home for Mother's Day and I needed an excuse. I wanted to be with you.

REED. I'm not your mother!

ZENOBIA. I had to have a good reason not to go. You see, Mother's Day is very important to my father. It's his wedding anniversary, too. He even calls my mother Mother.

REED. That doesn't surprise me—he called me a steer.

ZENOBIA. Oh, don't be angry with me, Reed.

REED. I'm not angry—I'm just mildly incensed.

ZENOBIA. I love you so. Be kind to me. (*Puts her arms around him.*)

REED. I've already been kind to you. Have you no saturation point? (*Frees himself.*)

ZENOBIA. There's no need to get excited. There's a very simple way to settle this misunderstanding.

REED. How? Shoot myself?

ZENOBIA. No. Marry me.

REED. Are you on pot! If you are—get off of it.

ZENOBIA. Just in love, my wonderful darling. (*Clings to him again.*) Oh, Reed, I'll make a good wife. I got straight "A's" in Home Economics.

REED. Zenobia, little dove, I am far too fond of you to ruin your young life. Find a nice boy with straight "A's" in *Business* Economics.

ZENOBIA. (*Holding him fiercely.*) No! I want you. You—*you!* You!

REED. There's no need to be repetitious. One fatal stab is enough.

ZENOBIA. Do you know why my father named me Zenobia? Zenobia was a Queen. He liked that. And when she was captured, she was led away in chains of pure gold. Well, you've captured me, Reed, and I want to be chained to you for the rest of my life.

REED. Zenobia, the only gold I have is in my teeth.

ZENOBIA. Dad has the gold, darling. To him, Fort Knox is a substation.

REED. My sweet child—you wouldn't want a man who would sell his soul solely for security. I have too much pride.

ZENOBIA. I know—I know. That's why I love you so. You have ideals. (*Hugs him.*) You're like Lancelot—Tristan—Robert Redford.

REED. Nevertheless, I won't take tawdry financial advantage of you. There is only one thing for us to do honorably. That's for you to confess your duplicity to your father. I promise you, you'll feel better. Cleansed. (*The door chimes are heard.*) Oh, shit. What now!

ZENOBIA. Reed — it's Dad. If he finds me here, he won't believe a word I say. When he phoned, I told him I was in bed with a headache.

REED. To him, that means me.

ZENOBIA. What'll I do!

REED. Jump out a window.

ZENOBIA. Hide me. He'll kill both of us. You first.

REED. (*Points to bedroom.*) In there. Hide in the bathroom.

ZENOBIA. What if he wants to use it?

REED. Take a shower. (*She dashes out. Reed picks up some papers, puts a pencil in his mouth and assuming a casual pose, saunters to the door and opens it. Roberta enters carrying a paper bag.*)

ROBERTA. I brought lasagna. (*Crosses toward kitchen.*)

REED. Ingrid, things have suddenly changed!

ROBERTA. Roberta. Who's Ingrid?

REED. The maid. Roberta, I've unexpected company.

ROBERTA. That's all right. I have enough food for an army.

REED. That's about what I've got. We'll have to make our assignation some other time.

ROBERTA. But you need me tonight, Reed. Any word yet?

REED. Any what?

ROBERTA. About your mother.

REED. Who?

ROBERTA. The hospital. (*Stops at kitchen door.*)

REED. Oh, mother. Yes — they just called. Everything's fine. It was just a spastic colon.

ROBERTA. Oh, I'm glad. Well, I'll start dinner for you anyhow.

REED. It's not necessary, Roberta. I can face the night alone now. Besides, my hernia is acting up.

ROBERTA. No use wasting the lasagna. (*Goes into the kitchen.*)

REED. What have I done to deserve this? Don't answer. (*The bedroom door opens and Zenobia sticks her head out.*)

ZENOBIA. Are we alone?

REED. No. Go back behind the shower curtain.

ZENOBIA. The little boy wants a banana.

REED. Give him my razor to play with.

36

ZENOBIA. Who's here?

REED. Who isn't? Go back to the bathroom.

ZENOBIA. I can't. The little boy is on the toilet.

REED. What the hell is he doing on the toilet! Never mind. Get under the bed. See if you can find my cuff links. (*She has no sooner gone out than Roberta returns, tying an apron around her waist.*)

ROBERTA. Do you have any hot seasoning?

REED. What else? Roberta, I'm really not in the mood to eat. Put it in a doggie bag and find a dog.

ROBERTA. You might get hungry later. I'll just make it hot for you.

REED. I'm doing great, dear, without any help. I just want to go to bed.

ROBERTA. Good. I brought something else, Reed. (*Smiles.*)

REED. If it's garlic bread — find a pigeon.

ROBERTA. I brought my toothbrush.

REED. Then clean your teeth and go home, dear.

ROBERTA. No. I'll stay and bite you.

REED. Sweetie — one can't be sexy with a throbbing hernia. Besides, I've got company.

ROBERTA. When are they coming?

REED. They're already here. (*Points.*) In there — looking for my cuff links.

ROBERTA. Are you expecting more?

REED. God — I hope not.

ROBERTA. (*Puts her hands on his shoulders.*) Reed, I want to confess something.

REED. There's a Catholic church around the corner.

ROBERTA. I misled you this afternoon. I'm really not at all prudish. When I'm turned on, I'm a volcano.

REED. That's all I need — a volcano spitting ashes.

ROBERTA. Poopsie, your trouble is, you're not aware of the devastating flame you kindle. You sizzle. You're thermodynamic. Kiss me.

REED. I haven't shaved, dear.

ROBERTA. All the better — so wildly masculine. Kiss me.

REED. What about your lasagna?

ROBERTA. We're both warming up. Kiss me. It'll improve your appetite. (*Reed kisses her. She clings to him. The door chimes interrupt.*)

REED. Oh, shit! It's him. That maniac is back!

ROBERTA. Who?

REED. A man who killed a coyote. Roberta, there's a girl in my bedroom named Zenobia. Her father is fighting her mother for her custody and I'm trying to help her. Tell her not to come out. Stay with her. Comfort her.

ROBERTA. How?

REED. I don't care. Get in bed with her. Just stay out of sight.

ROBERTA. (*At door.*) What about my lasagna?

REED. God willing, I'll hold it on simmer. (*She has no sooner gone into the bedroom than Ingrid enters from the hall.*)

INGRID. Hi. I skipped the babysitting.

REED. Ingrid—that's asking too much. Go back and earn your pin money. And pin it in your bra.

INGRID. I'm back to earn my "A." "A" as in assignation.

REED. I *can't* grade you now, dear. My mother has just been taken to the hospital and I'm in no mood to promote your Honda.

INGRID. But you *are* in a mood where you need to be distracted. Well, I'm the distraction. (*Starts taking her clothes off.*) Did you get to my "Pornography in Greek Drama" yet?

REED. (*Starts pushing her clothes back at her.*) Ingrid—can't you understand. I couldn't concentrate.

INGRID. No need. All you *have* to do is relax. I'll do the concentrating.

REED. I'll give you an "A" anyhow, Ingrid! You're going to rip your pantyhose.

INGRID. I don't trust you. If I don't deliver now, you won't deliver later and Dad won't deliver my Honda.

REED. Look—I'll swear it on a Bible.

INGRID. No need. We have a gentleman's agreement.

REED. You'll only make me feel inadequate.

INGRID. That's what *you* think. (*Throws her dress aside.*) Here—let me help *you*. (*Starts to undress him.*)

REED. Ingrid—stop that. My mother may be dying. I need sedation—not stimulation. I've told you, you don't have to do this for me now!

INGRID. I'm not. I'm doing it for a four-door Honda.

REED. You can have my car.

INGRID. I've seen it—a tuna can with wheels.

REED. Look, Ingrid. I'm an idealist. I want to *care* about you first. And how can I *care* about you with my mother in intensive care?

INGRID. We made an honorable deal. Are you going to honor it?

REED. Tomorrow. Under the circumstances, I'll be a Judas to motherhood.

INGRID. Judas got thirty pieces of silver. All I'm asking is an "A."

REED. You'll get it for services rendered if you'll just put on your pantyhose and take the service elevator.

INGRID. If you don't go ahead and seduce me within two minutes, I'm going to the door and yell "Rape!" That'll fix your tenure.

REED. With your clothes off?

INGRID. I'll say you ripped them off.

REED. But they're not ripped.

INGRID. I'll rip them.

REED. You're not Polish. You're a Kikuyo. They were the Mau Mau. (*The conflict is resolved by the door chimes.*)

INGRID. Someone's at the door!

REED. I know. It's the grim reaper.

INGRID. That's what we call the *dean*. I'll be expelled. (*Grabs her clothes. She overlooks the pantyhose under a chair.*)

REED. Serves you right for betraying motherhood.

INGRID. *You* got me into this! What'll I do?

REED. Join the club. We're all playing Hide n' Seek. (*She starts for bedroom.*) No — no! Not in there — the floor's just been painted. (*Points.*) The kitchen.

INGRID. Where'll I hide?

REED. There's an oven.

INGRID. I'll put my clothes on as fast as I can.

REED. And put the lasagna on simmer. (*She dashes into kitchen.*) All I need here is a traffic light. Well, I'll have to face him sooner or later. (*Again he picks up some papers, puts a pencil in his mouth and saunters to open the door. Angie enters.*)

ANGIE. Am I late?

REED. Oh, no. You couldn't have timed it better.

ANGIE. (*Kisses him.*) I skipped judo class.

REED. Pity. Because the wrestling match has been called off.

ANGIE. What do you mean?

REED. It's a rough night. More than I can handle. You'll have to go back to your dorm.

ANGIE. I don't live in a dorm.

REED. Well, wherever you live.

ANGIE. I have a little apartment.

REED. Well, get back quick as you can — and dust something. (*Pushes her toward door.*)

ANGIE. I can't.

REED. What do you mean you can't? You can't dust?

ANGIE. My girlfriend got married today. I let them have my apartment tonight for their honeymoon.

REED. Tell them you've changed your mind.

ANGIE. They won't understand. (*Resists his pushing.*)

REED. They know what an emergency is, don't they?

ANGIE. That's why they got married.

REED. Why can't they go to a motel?

ANGIE. They're on a scholarship that only pays for education.

REED. Then join them. Have an orgy. *That's* an education. (*Pushes her toward door.*)

ANGIE. What's happened to you? You act like you're trying to get rid of me. This night was to be a night to remember.

REED. It already is.

ANGIE. (*Twists away.*) I even went home and wrote a poem about you.

REED. Put it in the mail.

ANGIE. Why waste a stamp. (*Takes it out.*)

REED. Give it to me — I'll frame it.

ANGIE. No. I want to read it to you — to show you how much I love you.

REED. I'll take your word — you don't have to put it in a poem.

ANGIE. Listen. Because this comes from my heart. (*Reads.*)
"Reed, oh, Reed
Heed my need."

REED. Fabulous. Terrific. I'll keep it in my Bible. (*Pushes her again.*)

ANGIE. That's not the *end!*

REED. Well, we're getting close.

ANGIE. (*Reads.*)
"Must I plead?"

REED. Must I?

ANGIE. (*Continues.*)

"Must I bleed?"

REED. I am.

ANGIE. (*Barges on.*)

"Oh, come to me."

REED. Angie—why don't you go to a nice private telephone booth and read me the rest as if the words were coming from heaven.

ANGIE. I haven't got a quarter. (*Unremitting.*)

"With passionate speed."

REED. Fabulous! It rhymes. Where's your car?

ANGIE. In the shop. I bent the fender. (*Marches on.*)

"For God has decreed."

REED. Dear—I have to get dressed. There's a faculty "P.P." meeting—Postgraduate Policy.

ANGIE. (*Undaunted.*)

"My poor hearts need."

REED. And I've got a splitting headache. Go down to the lobby and have the doorman call you a taxi.

ANGIE. You haven't got a doorman. (*Reads on.*)

"Will soon succeed

And my soul be freed

Oh Reed, oh Reed, oh Reed."

(*Looks up.*)

That's the finish.

REED. I'm right behind you. You've got to leave now, sweetheart. I'm overcome.

ANGIE. (*Hurt.*) No. You don't like my poem.

REED. No—no! I wanted to cry. I wish there were more. Go home and write more.

ANGIE. Reed, I've told you I have nowhere to go!

REED. Go to a movie.

ANGIE. I haven't got my glasses.

REED. (*Forces his on her.*) Use mine.

ANGIE. Well, this certainly isn't what I expected when I was taking a hot shower. (*With the glasses now on, she puts out a probing hand.*) Where is everybody?

REED. Don't quibble. They look great on you. (*Pushes her to door as they chime.*)

41

ANGIE. Someone is at the door!

REED. (*Looks heavenward.*) Oh, God — I'm sorry for all my sins. Give me a break. I'll donate a hundred bucks to saving Wayward Girls.

ANGIE. Who is it?

REED. Ask the mortician later.

ANGIE. Reed, I can't be caught in a bachelor's apartment at night. I have a mother.

REED. You should have jumped before the ship sank.

ANGIE. Who do you *think* it is?

REED. I think it just might be a hunter from Texas looking for a coyote.

ANGIE. What does he want?

REED. He's going to tan the hide.

ANGIE. (*Dashes toward bedroom.*) I'll wait in your bedroom.

REED. No — no! The kitchen. No — the *bed*room! (*The chimes ring again.*)

ANGIE. I'll get in bed and hide under the covers.

REED. You'll have company.

ANGIE. There's someone in there?

REED. There's a meeting of the Girl Scouts. Wait! Give me back my glasses!

ANGIE. You won't need them.

REED. I might. No one hits a man with glasses on. (*He grabs his glasses back.*)

ANGIE. My horoscope warned me this was no day for new relationships or to buy a dog. (*Goes into bedroom. The chimes ring insistently. Reed bites a pencil again and saunters to open the door. Hercules Homer Hunter enters.*)

REED. Oh, hi, Homer.

HUNTER. Where is she!

REED. Which one?

HUNTER. My little Queen.

REED. Mr. Hunter, I told you I do not allow any females in this celibate domicile. Why there hasn't even been a hairpin here since — when was Lincoln shot?

HUNTER. You think I'd take the word of a eunuch?

REED. Not even on a Bible?

HUNTER. Not even on the Boston Cook Book. In *Boston*.

REED. Why would your daughter be here, sir? I don't hold night classes.

HUNTER. That's just what I want to find out.

REED. I never allow students here after dusk. It sets a low moral tone when the sun sets.

HUNTER. She's not in her dorm room.

REED. Maybe she's out jogging. Who knows?

HUNTER. For all I know, she may be in your bedroom right now.

REED. Mr. Hunter, I can no longer tolerate this invasion of my privacy. If you do not desist, I shall have to call the police. (*Picks up phone.*)

HUNTER. You do that. I just may want to bring charges against you.

REED. (*Puts phone down.*) On second thought, I may be able to help you find her. Does she have a car?

HUNTER. What do you think we do in Texas—walk?

REED. Well, it just occurred to me she might have decided to drive home to surprise you.

HUNTER. It's too long a drive. I'd have sent one of my Lear jets for her.

REED. You own a jet?

HUNTER. I own Dallas.

REED. Is it expensive? Owning a jet—not Dallas.

HUNTER. You're trying to get rid of me. That means only one thing. You're expecting her to show up.

REED. May God strike me dead if that's true.

HUNTER. Well, I wouldn't take insurance on that. So, I'm going to sit here and wait and if she shows up at this launching pad, there's going to be one mighty sorry eunuch. (*Sits down solidly.*)

REED. They're usually sorry anyhow but that's beside the point. Look, sir, I will swear on my Bible—my real Bible—that I haven't the faintest idea where you daughter is at *this* moment. Wait. (*Looks around.*) Now, where is that new Bible! I belong to a book club. (*Gives up search for it. Hunter looks down and picks up a pair of pantyhose.*)

HUNTER. Never mind your Holy Bible. I've just had a revelation.

REED. Well, if you're willing to take the word of a eunuch. (*Stands back.*)

HUNTER. (*Holds up pantyhose.*) What does this look like to you, son?

REED. (*Comes down, takes pantyhose and examines it solemnly.*) I'd say it's some sort of feminine apparel, wouldn't you?

HUNTER. And just how do you think it got here?

REED. I don't know. Did you bring it?

HUNTER. I found it under that chair. Is this something eunuchs wear?

REED. Not to the best of my knowledge.

HUNTER. Then explain how it got here.

REED. (*Hits his forehead.*) Of course! I remember! When my sister was here today, she changed clothes before going back to the convent.

HUNTER. They wear pantyhose in a convent?

REED. They're very liberal Dominicans.

HUNTER. Well, I'm *not*.

REED. Which?

HUNTER. Neither. And I think there's someone in that room wearing a single nylon. And furthermore, I intend to find out. It just better not be my Queen Zenobia with the naked leg.

REED. (*Races to door to block him, arms outstretched.*) Over my dead body.

HUNTER. You said it—I didn't. (*He takes out his revolver.*)

REED. (*Crosses to him cautiously, one palm outstretched to stop a bullet.*) Now look, Mr. Hunter. I'm sorry I didn't explain before. I've a very sick aunt in there with a nurse and a thyroidectomy. She can't be disturbed. She's ninety-one.

HUNTER. She wear pantyhose?

REED. Besides the door is locked.

HUNTER. Then give me the key.

REED. I haven't got it.

HUNTER. Who has it?

REED. The painter.

HUNTER. Where's the painter?

REED. Home.

HUNTER. Why'd he take the key?

REED. Drunk.

HUNTER. What if you had to get in? Or out?

REED. I've sent for a locksmith.

HUNTER. When'll he get here?

REED. Within the hour. Why don't we sit down and review your problem like two rational human beings, Homer? Nothing was ever resolved by impetuosity. Would you like a drink? A stinger? A bloody mary?

HUNTER. I don't intend to *wait*.

REED. Oh. May I call you a taxi, sir?

HUNTER. I'm going to blow that lock off. (*Aims revolver at Reed.*) Now, stand back. I've six bullets in this. You want to pick a number?

REED. Seven. Please, Mister Hunter. I've Puerto Rican neighbors above me. They're very nervous about gunfire.

HUNTER. (*Points at door and shouts.*) Now hear this. Now hear *this*. If anybody's in that bedroom, they better come out hands up or feet first. Because when I count to three — I start shooting. One. Two.

REED. Two and a half. Wait!

HUNTER. Three! (*Behind him, Ingrid comes out of the kitchen fully dressed.*)

INGRID. I put the lasagna on simmer. (*Hunter whirls around as the bedroom door opens and Vanessa and Roberta and Angie file out. Zenobia is last.*)

HUNTER. What the hell are you running here — a harem?

ZENOBIA. (*Recovers her wits.*) Daddy! What a surprise. (*Runs to embrace him.*)

REED. Yes! (*Suddenly inspired.*) Surprise! (*Urges everyone to join in.*) Surprise! It's his wedding anniversary. Surprise — everybody!

HUNTER. What the hell —

REED. You almost spoiled the surprise party — you Dallas devil you.

ZENOBIA. Yes! It's for you, Daddy. Surprise. (*Everyone shouts "Surprise."*)

REED. You certainly gave me a bad time trying to keep it secret, sir.

ZENOBIA. We planned it for you, Daddy — it's *your* day?

HUNTER. Mother's Day?

ZENOBIA. Your wedding anniversary.

REED. And your daughter begged me to help plan this party

45

for you. Where's the food? Bring on the lasagna. (*Roberta dashes into kitchen.*)

HUNTER. Well, you sure fooled me.

ZENOBIA. And these are all my classmates—to wish you a Happy Anniversary.

HUNTER. (*To Vanessa.*) You a student?

VANESSA. I teach philosophy. (*The boy comes out of the bedroom.*)

BOY. I want a banana.

HUNTER. Where'd *he* come from?

VANESSA. Hocapocapoo.

HUNTER. He in college?

REED. A prodigy.

ZENOBIA. And you almost spoiled everything with your suspicions. Shame on you, Daddy Pooh.

HUNTER. (*Puts his arm around her.*) I guess that sort of makes me a fool, don't it?

REED. You said it—I didn't.

ZENOBIA. But we all forgive you, Daddy.

REED. You should be very proud of her, sir. She's brilliant.

ZENOBIA. And isn't Professor Dolan a dear, Daddy?

VANESSA. A genius.

ROBERTA. (*Returns from kitchen with a smoking dish.*) The lasagna's burned.

REED. Now isn't that life for you. Our plans are never controlled by the controllable but the uncontrollable.

VANESSA. I wish I'd said that.

ZENOBIA. Well, the party isn't spoiled, Daddy, why don't you take *all of us* out for a celebration dinner. We can still have our party for you.

HUNTER. Well, I'll do just that. Wait a minute—how'd you know *I'd* be here?

ZENOBIA. That's why I wrote I was engaged, silly. I know your curiosity.

HUNTER. I guess I'm a stupid coyote.

REED. You said it—I didn't.

HUNTER. Alright, everybody. Out! I'm taking all you nice folks to a fancy restaurant for a feast you're going to remember until the Republicans get back in.

VANESSA. That long?

ZENOBIA. Oh, *thank* you, Professor Dolan—for everything.

REED. My pleasure.

HUNTER. (*To Reed.*) You coming?

REED. I wish I could but I've students to grade. Duty first.

VANESSA. And I have an urgent problem to solve.

REED. But would you like for me to recommend a very good restaurant?

HUNTER. Nope. I got my own favorite restaurant. A very fancy place called "The Arm Pit."

REED. Sounds fancy?

HUNTER. Sure is. Got topless waitresses.

REED. Must be difficult to keep your mind on your liver.

HUNTER. Good beef, tho.

REED. (*Goes with him to door.*) I don't believe I know it.

HUNTER. Why should you? It's in Dallas. (*To hallway.*) Everybody to the airport! (*Goes out.*)

REED. (*Closes door.*) Wow! I want a drink! (*Starts for bar.*)

BOY. I want a banana.

REED. Can't you keep him quiet for a minute? He's getting an oral perversion about his banana.

VANESSA. Then show him a little paternal concern. After all these fruitless years, you owe him a banana.

REED. Where am I going to get a banana at this time of night! Panama?

VANESSA. You're a genius. A banana should be easy after the miracle you just pulled.

REED. All right! All right. I've a friend here owns the penthouse and a jacuzzi. (*Starts for door.*) Maybe *she* has a banana. (*He goes out.*)

BOY. I don't like him.

VANESSA. You don't know him. He can be very sweet.

BOY. He smells bad.

VANESSA. Bachelors sometimes do, dear. They don't have wives to wash and dry them out.

BOY. I want to go home.

VANESSA. (*Looks at her watch.*) Alright—I'll send you home to your mother, dear. My time is up anyhow. (*Goes to card table and takes out checkbook.*) I only rented you till now.

BOY. Why was I pretending he was my father?

VANESSA. I was teaching him a long overdue lesson.

47

BOY. Was he naughty?

VANESSA. (*Writing check.*) That depends on one's perspective—one's age and urge.

BOY. What'd he do?

VANESSA. You'd only be interested if you were older.

BOY. Were *you* naughty?

VANESSA. Again, that depends on your perspective and retrospect.

BOY. I don't know what that means.

VANESSA. You will—someday. (*Hands him a check.*) Give this check to your mother and thank her for lending you to me. It's to go toward your education.

BOY. Did I do good?

VANESSA. Perfect. You'll probably end up a movie star.

BOY. (*Eagerly.*) And kill people?

VANESSA. Dozens. And a few lovely ladies, too. Now hurry. Your mother is due to pick you up in the lobby.

BOY. Will she take me to a movie?

VANESSA. Why not? You've earned it. There's a good picture for children at Cinema Two.

BOY. What's it about?

VANESSA. A tender love story of incest. (*Kisses him.*) I only wish you *were* mine.

BOY. See you around, pardner. (*He goes out. Vanessa is pensive for a moment. She lights a cigarette. She takes a hair ribbon from her purse, looks at it and puts it back. Reed returns with a grapefruit which he tosses to Vanessa.*)

REED. Peel this. It's all she had. Where's the midget monster?

VANESSA. He's gone.

REED. Gone?

VANESSA. You'll never see him again, Reed.

REED. What do you mean—he's dead?

VANESSA. I sent him home.

REED. That was very sensible. Now, we can sit down and decide calmly how you should raise the kid.

VANESSA. How *we* should raise the kid.

REED. (*Sits and holds her hands.*) Vannie, dear, you just had a perfect demonstration of what my scholastic life is like here. So many of these girls throw themselves at me I can't keep a suit pressed. I suppose they're looking for a cushy career as a professor's wife. Oh, they're devious! Believe me, it's a daily hazard to be a bachelor in a coeducational cohabiting college.

VANESSA. I know. While I was in your bedroom, the girls told me about your celibate life. You'll undoubtedly be canonized.

REED. Didn't I *tell* you they were devious!

VANESSA. Diabolical. Poor nymphets.

REED. A college is no atmosphere in which to raise a future president. You should take him to a more conducive climate.

VANESSA. Geographically or morally?

REED. Someplace where he'll develop into a man worthy of us both. He can learn to *ski* in *Switzerland.*

VANESSA. Reed, I want to tell you something before you become hopelessly entangled in your own self-deception. I loved you once. And I never got over it. I want you to know that.

REED. (*Takes her hands.*) Oh, Vanessa, sweetheart — I loved you, too. And I never recovered either. *That's* why I never married.

VANESSA. Would you kindly have the grace and good manners to cut the shit?

REED. Vanessa! Vulgarity doesn't become a saint.

VANESSA. Nor deception. So I'm going to confess what I've done. I came back today to find out something.

REED. (*Trying to take her hands.*) With the living testament of our love.

VANESSA. Must I be vulgar again? As I said, I never got over you. Like sinus. (*Rises to pace.*) Oh, I married but it didn't banish you as I'd hoped. You were still in my blood.

REED. (*Sits looking up at her.*) Dear Vannie.

VANESSA. After I lost my husband I devised a plan to find out if you were still the boy I loved — or a man I still might want.

REED. Both — I hope.

VANESSA. So I produced a son.

REED. *We* produced a son. Together.

VANESSA. I wanted to test you — to see if you would react like a frightened youth or a responsible adult that I could love and respect.

REED. You needn't worry, Vanessa. I'm not going to fail you. I'll send you a check for child support every month. Certified.

VANESSA. And you fell flat on your ass.

REED. Vanessa — you're a mother!

49

VANESSA. Would that I were. But I'm not. (*Stops and faces him.*) That little boy wasn't your son. I *rented* him.

REED. (*Digests this.*) I have a *rented* son?

VANESSA. You have no son at all.

REED. You mean you deliberately misled me.

VANESSA. Just as you did me ten years ago.

REED. Who's kid is he, then?

VANESSA. He's the son of a friend of mine. Isn't that a relief?

REED. (*He is silent a moment.*) No. I was beginning to like the kid.

VANESSA. Oh my God—you're a chameleon—you change color *instantly* with every new background. Don't you ever have a sense of guilt?

REED. What have I done wrong?

VANESSA. You deceive—you misrepresent—you distort—you evade—you pretend and you lie with the innocence of a naughty child with jam on his face.

REED. Look what *you've* just done—deceiving me.

VANESSA. My motives were not selfish.

REED. What else were they?

VANESSA. Oh, no. You're not going to turn the tables on *me*. May I tell you what you are in one word?

REED. It's four words, isn't it?

VANESSA. Your exotic, idiotic love of the erotic is like a hypnotic narcotic, both neurotic and psychotic. There. One word.

REED. (*Grins.*) Would you repeat that please.

VANESSA. Oh, I'm going. (*Starts for door.*)

REED. Wait a minute. Every criminal has a right for rebuttal. At least grant me that "inch of time" to defend myself.

VANESSA. Oh, this is going to be good. (*Returns.*)

REED. I grant you—I *do* sometimes resort to deception—just as you did.

VANESSA. Sometimes? The truth is anathema to you. For you, it's not a thing to embrace—it's something to embroider.

REED. No. I embellish to enhance. I try to make life a little less harsh for those I love. I don't like to see people angry or unhappy. I try to avoid pain. You'd do that for a headache, wouldn't you?

VANESSA. Which I'm rapidly getting.

REED. A little deception is no egregious sin, Vanessa.

50

VANESSA. It is when you make it into a monumental virtue. I'm leaving.

REED. Wait . . . Do you wear lipstick?

VANESSA. Did I leave it?

REED. Or false eyelashes?

VANESSA. Of course.

REED. Wear a bra?

VANESSA. *You* should know that.

REED. Do those little deceptions hurt anyone?

VANESSA. Of course not.

REED. Well, that's all I do. (*Walks away.*)

VANESSA. You wear lipstick?

REED. I try to make things a little more attractive.

VANESSA. (*Storms back at him.*) *You are a born manipulator.* (*Backs him up, jabbing her finger into his chest.*) If you were only crooked instead of adolescently amorous, you would make millions—instead of giddy gullible girls.

REED. (*Grins.*) Like you.

VANESSA. You catch yourself in your own traps and then wiggle out with the dexterity of a Houdini.

REED. Who Houdini? (*Tries to put his arms around her.*)

VANESSA. (*Now retreating as he continues to fondle her.*) You're the only man I know who could hitchhike back if he were left on the moon.

REED. I wouldn't want to—if you were with me. (*Vanessa struggles to free herself.*)

VANESSA. Or, if you had been a lawyer, you could have exonerated Hitler. (*Slaps his hands away.*) Immortalized Mussolini.

REED. She loves me. (*Fights to embrace her.*)

VANESSA. Made Nero a hero. (*Fights him off.*)

REED. She wants me. (*Continues the struggle.*)

VANESSA. Saved Satan.

REED. She's mad for me. (*He manages to pin her arm down.*)

VANESSA. Justified Judas. (*He holds her in a tight embrace and kisses her. When she is released, she sinks back on the sofa.*) Who was it said—Every woman has to have one bastard in her life?

REED. (*Uses his grin.*) Eighteen carat.

VANESSA. I don't know whether to laugh or cry. Or cut my wrists.

REED. Don't do that. I faint at the sight of blood.

VANESSA. Tell me the truth, just once — before I leave. Why didn't you answer my letters?

REED. (*Sits beside her.*) I couldn't offer you anything. I had a bedridden mother to support. I decided the quick cut was the kindest. Like any good surgeon — one must cut to cure.

VANESSA. Thank you. I feel better. (*Rises.*)

REED. Don't go, Vannie. Not yet. Let's have a final drink together.

VANESSA. I don't know. I remember last time — the first time.

REED. Just a friendly suicide pact.

VANESSA. No. I have a plane to catch.

REED. Just one ittsie bittsie drink? As the Bible says — "Futility reapeth a barren harvest." Deuteronomy.

VANESSA. Well . . . just *one* . . . while I make up my face. I seem to have lost it. (*Takes out pact.*)

REED. (*Goes to bar.*) I'd like you to believe me when I tell you this, Vanessa, that if it weren't for my mother being so ill, I'd beg you to marry me. Think of what a happy married couple we'd make.

VANESSA. Yes . . . we'd never go to bed angry. We'd stay up and fight.

REED. (*Surreptitiously adds to drink.*) You really blew it, dear, when you walked out on me. You never gave yourself a chance to find out how sweet I can be.

VANESSA. I'm sure you're delectable . . . a steamy dish of sweet and sour pork.

REED. The spice of life. (*Returns with drinks. He sits beside her.*) Well . . . here's to Hocapocapoo and that youthful . . . lyrical . . . innocent consummation.

VANESSA. Innocent! I was so innocent I thought "consumate" was a dirty word.

REED. It is . . . for others. Here's to us . . . babes in the woods.

VANESSA. "Out of the woods" and into the hay . . . which turned out to be a polar bear rug.

REED. And so very, very young . . . so piteously . . . poignantly . . . young. (*He covers her hands with his.*)

VANESSA. (*Turns to face him.*) Reed, tell me the truth . . . if you can manage it for a change. Why haven't you ever married? Really.

REED. I told you. You spoiled all other women for me.

VANESSA. (*Jerks her hands away.*) Oh, Reed, stop it! Let me leave with a modicum of respect for your sagacity . . . if you know what it means.

REED. I can't even spell it. But it's true.

VANESSA. Will you swear that on a Bible?

REED. I thought you'd never ask. (*Rises to take oath.*) And those letters I never answered. I still have them locked up.

VANESSA. Get them.

REED. (*Taps his heart.*) They're here. Now, where'd I put my mother's old Bible? (*Searches upstage. Vanessa remains on sofa.*) Ah—here it is. (*He puts hand on book.*) I, Reed Victor Dolan, do solemnly hereby swear on this Holy Bible that when you, Vanessa, went out of my life—the life went out of me.

VANESSA. Oh, Reed—I'm so touched. (*Takes out her handkerchief and dabs her eyes.*) When I think of what might have been.

REED. And still could be. (*Sits beside her again.*)

VANESSA. My God—this drink is strong. I'm acting like a fool—does that surprise you?

REED. You're acting like an angel which doesn't surprise me at all. (*Takes handkerchief from her.*) What a wonderful perfume. What is it? "Lust?"

VANESSA. Of course not. It's called "Rememberance."

REED. Could anything be more appropriate? "Remember-ance." I love it.

VANESSA. I'll send you some.

REED. We've so much to remember, haven't we, Vanessa?

VANESSA. Wait. Here, hold my drink. (*Opens her purse and takes out a ribbon.*) I wonder if you'll remember this. I've saved it all these wasted years. Ever see this before?

REED. Yes! You wore it in your hair—at Hocapocapoo.

VANESSA. And do you remember what you did with it that night?

REED. (*Stalls.*) How could I forget?

VANESSA. Well, if you did, you'd be embarrassed. You really were a rascal to shock me like that—coming in nude from the shower with this ribbon tied in a lovely bow around your—

your — (*Covers her face with her handkerchief.*)

REED. I didn't!

VANESSA. You did.

REED. Not that!

VANESSA. Yes — *that*. I'd never seen one before. (*Covers her eyes.*)

REED. Even in a museum?

VANESSA. It's not quite the same.

REED. And you saved it?

VANESSA. (*Blushes — if possible.*) What would my mother think if she knew?

REED. Why did you save it?

VANESSA. I don't know. Some people save their kidney stones. Frugal, I guess.

REED. But you saved it . . . when you might have used it to tie up some Christmas present.

VANESSA. After where that had been! God would have struck me dead.

REED. Vannie Pannie, let that ribbon tie us together again.

VANESSA. What do you mean?

REED. Give it to me. Stay here. I'll show you.

VANESSA. Reed, what are you going to do?

REED. Guess. (*He rises and dangles the ribbon in the air.*)

VANESSA. Reed! Really. What are you! Some sort of academic exhibitionist!

REED. (*Nods.*) Extracurricular.

VANESSA. Well, I'm not curious anymore. I've seen all those movies! And I'm *not* staying. I have that plane to catch.

REED. (*Pushes her back.*) There's another tomorrow *morning*.

VANESSA. (*Rises.*) I've a dental appointment.

REED. (*Pushes her back.*) Your appointment is here — with destiny.

VANESSA. (*Rises.*) Reed — you can't. I will not allow you to parade nude on Mother's Day.

REED. Sweetheart, I'm only going to recreate those dear sweet innocent memories of Hocapocapoo. (*Pushes her back. She stays put.*)

VANESSA. That was ten years ago!

REED. Nothing's changed. (*Goes to bedroom door.*) Everything's the same. I won't disappoint you.

VANESSA. Well, I'm not going to disappoint my dentist. (*Rises.*) *I'm* leaving.

REED. Relax. Fix yourself a drink. I'll only take a minute.

VANESSA. Reed! Be sensible. A red ribbon is not an aphrodisiac.

REED. Of course not. Nor is the moon or a polar bear rug. (*Opens door.*) I hope I can still tie a bow knot. (*He goes out.*)

VANESSA. Reed! Come back. You're being silly. Well, *I'm* not going to stay. It's too embarrassing. (*Storms to the door. And stops.*) On the other hand. Oh, what the hell. You've seen one — you've seen them all. (*Returns to sofa and takes off her jacket.*) As the man said — futility reapeth a barren harvest. (*She goes up to the bar to fix herself a drink. As she returns, she discovers the Boston Cookbook. She looks toward the bedroom and sighs. She opens the pages and reads.*) "Sweet and Sour Pork." (*She closes the book and takes it down to the sofa. She finds a pad and quickly writes a note. She puts it in the cookbook and places the book in the center of the sofa. She then picks up her jacket and goes to the door. She gives a last look backward, sighs and goes out. After a moment, the bedroom door opens outward. Unseen, Reed gives an imitation bugle announcement before entering. He then appears in his bathrobe, wearing a wide grin.*)

REED. Hocapocapoo rides again! (*He looks around the room.*) Vanessa? (*When there is no answer, he crosses up to the kitchen door and looks in.*) Vanessa? O.K., sweetie. You want to play hide and seek the way we did before? *I'll* play with you! Anytime. (*He goes down to the end of the sofa and hides behind the end on his hands and knees.*) Try and find me. Come out — come out — wherever you are. Your little red ribbon is tied in place! Find me and untie it — just like good old Hocapocapoo. (*When no one appears, he stands puzzled a moment, then sees the cookbook. He picks it up. He finds the note and reads it aloud.*) "Once a shit — always a shit." (*He hurls the book toward the wall, knocking a picture down. He goes to retrieve it and stumbles over a foot stool — "flat on his face." He raises on his elbow.*) Shit! (*Since the prophecy is now fulfilled.*)

THE CURTAIN FALLS ALSO

QUOTATION IN LATIN

Deo teste meo, ut Johannus Baptistus Poquelinis hinc ad
munus suppelectilis regalis instruendae designaretur de manu
ipsa ego Ludivicus tredecimus, rex Galliae decrevi.

TRUE TRANSLATION

God bear witness that Jean-Baptiste Poquelin is hereby ap-
pointed Royal Upholsterer by the hand of Louis XIII, King of
France.

PROPERTY LIST

ACT I
Card table & chair
Term papers
Horn-rimmed glasses
Cocktail glasses
Sofa telephone
Wall telephone
Bar bottles
Door chimes
Jacket
Manuscript folder
Manuscript
Cookbook
Sofa pillows
Cigarettes
Lighter
Date book
Ice bucket

ACT II
Molière script
Pencils
Paper bag
Apron
Reading glasses
Pantyhose
Revolver
Smoking dish
Hair ribbon
Grapefruit
Handkerchief
Bathrobe
Written note
Footstool
Watch (Vanessa)
Checkbook (Vanessa)
Pad of paper

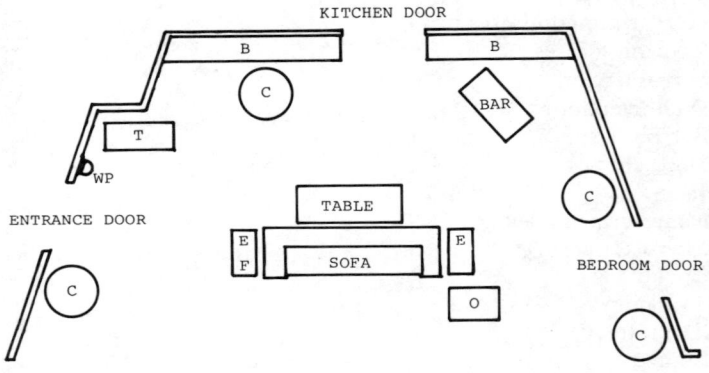

B   book shelves
C   chairs
E   end tables
F   table phone
O   ottoman
T   tables
WP   wall phone

The Reluctant Rogue

RECENT

Acquisitions

HOW I GOT THAT STORY
THE BUTLER DID IT
TERRA NOVA
GREAT SOLO TOWN
FATHER DREAMS
TERROR BY GASLIGHT
LAUNDRY AND BOURBON
EL HERMANO
CACCIATORE (3 short plays)
THE GREAT
   LABOR DAY CLASSIC
DAVID MAMET: SHORT PLAYS
   AND MONOLOGUES

*Write for information as to
availability*

TITLES

CRIMES OF THE HEART
KEY EXCHANGE
THE HOTHOUSE
EINSTEIN AND THE POLAR BEAR
THE GOOD PARTS
GARDENIA
THE NERD
TWELVE DREAMS
GHOSTS OF THE LOYAL OAKS
DEAD GIVEAWAY
ONE MONKEY DON'T STOP NO SHOW
THE GROVES OF ACADEME &
    THE PLUMBER'S APPRENTICE
THE ROADS TO HOME

● *Write for Information*

DRAMATISTS PLAY SERVICE, INC.

440 Park Avenue South   New York, N.Y. 10016

New

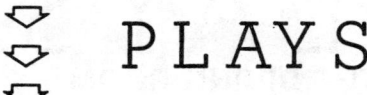 PLAYS

MASS APPEAL
LYDIE BREEZE
LOLITA
THE FANTOD
BILLY IRISH
GENERAL GORGEOUS
OPERATION MIDNIGHT CLIMAX
TIES
PASSING THROUGH
ANDROMACHE
DUMPING GROUND
CONFLUENCE & THE SKIRMISHERS
THE EYE OF THE BEHOLDER

INQUIRIES INVITED

 DRAMATISTS PLAY SERVICE, INC.
440 Park Avenue South   New York, N. Y. 10016

New
PLAYS

THE DINING ROOM

THE WEST SIDE WALTZ

**THE LIFE AND ADVENTURES
OF NICHOLAS NICKLEBY**

SOMETHING CLOUDY, SOMETHING CLEAR

THE HOTEL PLAY

FRANKENSTEIN

THREADS

DARK RIDE

ELEGY FOR A LADY

TITANIC

AM I BLUE

THE UNDEFEATED RHUMBA CHAMP

DRAMATISTS PLAY SERVICE, INC.
440 PARK AVENUE SOUTH   NEW YORK, N.Y. 10016

NEW Plays

'NIGHT, MOTHER
WHAT I DID LAST SUMMER
FEEDLOT
A DIFFERENT MOON
DOMESTIC ISSUES
DADDIES
THE HOUSE OF SLEEPING BEAUTIES
WIN/LOSE/DRAW
SLACKS AND TOPS
THE ART OF SELF-DEFENSE
TIME FRAMED
FLIGHT LINES & CROSSINGS

DRAMATISTS PLAY SERVICE, INC.
440 PARK AVENUE SOUTH   **NEW YORK, N.Y. 10016**

New
PLAYS

ANGELS FALL

THE WAKE OF JAMEY FOSTER

CHRISTMAS ON MARS

THE VALUE OF NAMES

LAST LOOKS

ASIAN SHADE

FOB

SOME KIND OF LOVE STORY

BUDDIES

EARLY WARNINGS

BARTOK AS DOG

THE GREAT AMERICAN CHEESE SANDWICH

Inquiries Invited

DRAMATISTS PLAY SERVICE, INC.

440 Park Avenue South   New York, N. Y. 10016